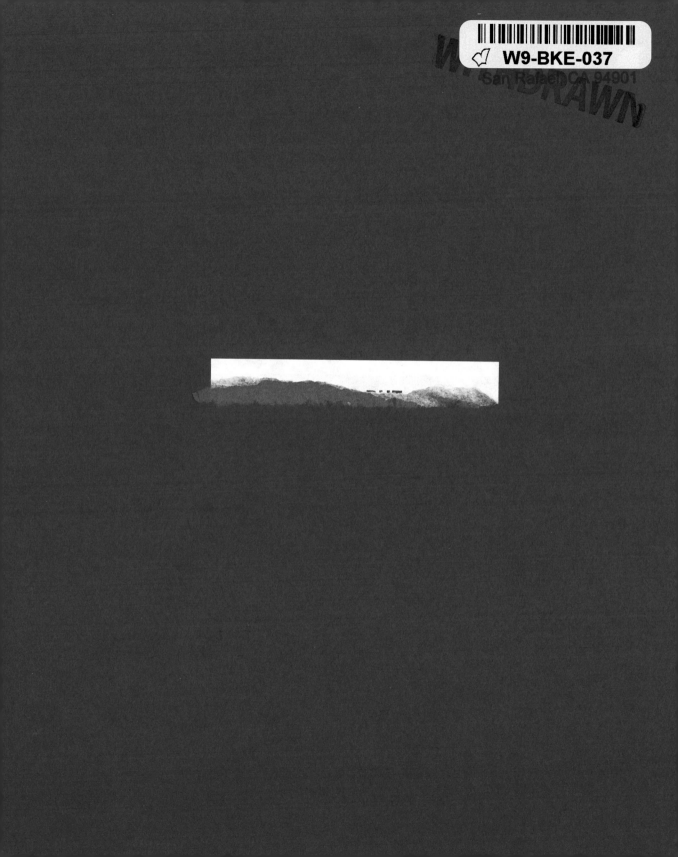

The Reconstruction Amendments

by Michael Burgan

Content Adviser: Kurt Hackemer, Ph.D.,
Department of History
University of South Dakota

Reading Adviser: Susan Kesselring, M.A.,
Literacy Educator,
Rosemount–Apple Valley–Eagan (Minnesota) School District

COMPASS POINT BOOKS
MINNEAPOLIS, MINNESOTA

Compass Point Books
3109 West 50th Street, #115
Minneapolis, MN 55410

Visit Compass Point Books on the Internet at *www.compasspointbooks.com*
or e-mail your request to *custserv@compasspointbooks.com*

On the cover: Hand colored illustration from an 1867 drawing by Alfred R. Waud of African-Americans going to the polls for the first state election during Reconstruction

Photographs ©: Bettmann/Corbis, cover, 13; Prints Old & Rare, back cover (far left); Library of Congress, back cover, 7, 8, 14, 22, 23, 25, 41; The Granger Collection, New York, 5, 16, 20, 27, 32, 37, 39; North Wind Picture Archives, 11, 18, 38; National Archives and Records Administration, 12, 35; MPI/Getty Images, 17; Corbis, 28.

Editor: Julie Gassman
Page Production: Bobbie Nuytten
Photo Researcher: Svetlana Zhurkin
Cartographer: XNR Productions, Inc.
Library Consultant: Kathleen Baxter

Creative Director: Keith Griffin
Editorial Director: Carol Jones
Managing Editor: Catherine Neitge

Library of Congress Cataloging-in-Publication Data
Burgan, Michael.
  The Reconstruction amendments / by Michael Burgan.
      p. cm.—(We the people)
  Includes bibliographical references and index.
  ISBN 0-7565-1636-6 (hard cover)
1. United States. Constitution. 13th-15th Amendments—Juvenile literature. 2. Constitutional amendments—United States—Juvenile literature. 3. Civil rights—United States—History—Juvenile literature. 4. Slavery—Law and legislation—United States—Juvenile literature.
5. Reconstruction (U.S. history, 1865-1877)—Juvenile literature. I. Title. II. We the people (Series) (Compass Point Books)
  KF4757.Z9B87 2006
    342.7303—dc22   2005025088

TABLE OF CONTENTS

A NATION DIVIDED

The year was 1865. The Civil War had been raging for nearly four years. Eleven Southern states had sparked the war when they seceded, or broke away, from the United States to form their own nation. Northern troops had fought these states, known as the Confederacy, to keep them in the Union.

Many bloody battles had been fought. But the end of the war was nearing. In April 1865, Confederate Army General Robert E. Lee realized his men could not go on. He surrendered to Ulysses S. Grant, commander of the Union Army. The Civil War would soon be over.

When the war began in 1861, some Northerners favored the abolition of slavery. Many others wanted to prevent its expansion into the new Western states. Southerners, however, wanted to keep slavery. The South relied on African-American slaves to run its economy. Southern slave owners feared that U.S. President Abraham

4

Lincoln would try to end slavery in the South, even though he had said he would not do so.

Southerners pointed to the U.S. Constitution in their arguments for slavery. This document was created in 1787 to outline the basic form of the U.S. government. It protects the rights of U.S. citizens and the individual states. The South argued that according to the Constitution, Lincoln had no legal right to limit slavery or to end slavery

General Lee surrendered to General Grant at Appomattox Court House in Virginia.

where it already existed. Not trusting Lincoln to follow the Constitution, the slave states of the South seceded. Lincoln said the Constitution did not allow states to secede. He fought the Civil War to keep the Union together.

Even before the Civil War ended, Congress called for a new amendment to the Constitution. In 1864, the lawmakers proposed the 13th Amendment, which outlawed slavery everywhere in the United States. During the next five years, Congress and the states would pass two more amendments that protected the rights of African-Americans.

The 13th, 14th, and 15th Amendments to the Constitution were part of a larger program called Reconstruction. Northern lawmakers started reconstructing, or rebuilding, the states of Louisiana and Tennessee in 1863. By the time the war ended, the Reconstruction effort extended to the other Southern states, which had suffered great damage during the war.

In addition to rebuilding cities, the lawmakers

hoped to reconstruct Southern society. They wanted to protect the rights of blacks and help them play a role in the governments of the Southern states.

Reconstruction led to many heated debates within Congress. The three related amendments were part of those arguments. But in the end, the Reconstruction Amendments helped shape a nation trying to restore order after a bloody civil war.

An 1865 photograph shows destruction from the Civil War in Richmond, Virginia.

7

FREEING THE SLAVES

As the Civil War began, President Lincoln saw how the issue of slavery had divided the nation. He believed that blacks deserved the same legal rights as whites. The most basic right was to control their own lives, something they could not do as slaves. A year into the war, Lincoln told several members of his Cabinet, "We must free the slaves or be ourselves subdued."

The issue, however, was not an easy one. Four states that allowed slavery had remained loyal to the Union. Lincoln did not want to lose the support

President Abraham Lincoln

8

of slave owners in Delaware, Kentucky, Maryland, and Missouri. He decided to first emancipate, or free, slaves in those Southern states that were rebelling against the U.S. government. Lincoln's Emancipation Proclamation of 1863 was the national government's first effort to end slavery.

But some Americans questioned whether the Emancipation Proclamation was constitutional. In order to settle the issue, Lincoln supported an amendment to the Constitution that would abolish slavery. The 13th Amendment would extend emancipation to the entire Union. And because amendments are permanent, Congress would never be able to pass laws that allowed slavery in any form.

The amendment was supported by Lincoln's political party, the Republicans. This party controlled Congress during and after the Civil War. Throughout much of the Reconstruction period, the Republicans also ran most Southern state governments.

The other major party was the Democrats, who

opposed the amendment. Many Democrats agreed with Southerners that states had a constitutional right to allow slavery. In addition, some Northern Democrats feared that abolishing slavery would make it impossible for the North and South to ever have good relations. They thought Southerners would remain angry with Northerners for ending something that was so important to them.

Under the U.S. Constitution, two-thirds of the members of both the Senate and the House of Representatives must vote for a proposed amendment. When the 13th Amendment came up for a vote in the Senate, there were enough Republicans to easily pass it.

The House, however, was a different story. The first time the House voted on the amendment, enough Democrats voted against the bill that it was defeated. But by January 1865, most Democrats realized that Northern voters wanted to end slavery. The lawmakers feared they might lose the support of those voters if they blocked the amendment. So with some Democratic support, the House

The House of Representatives celebrates the passing of the 13th Amendment in 1865.

finally approved the 13th Amendment. Pleased by the amendment's progress, Lincoln said, "This amendment is a King's cure for all the evils. It winds the whole thing up."

Under the Constitution, three-quarters of the states must also ratify, or approve, an amendment for it to take effect. By the end of 1865, enough states had

11

The original document stating the 13th Amendment, which abolished slavery and became law in December 1865

ratified the 13th Amendment for it to become part of the Constitution. The issue that had led to the Civil War would never be a problem again.

BATTLE IN WASHINGTON, D.C.

Although slavery had been abolished, lawmakers in the South soon created laws to limit the rights of newly freed slaves. The laws were called Black Codes. Each state had its own codes. The South Carolina code, for example, said black laborers had to live on their employer's property and needed the employer's permission to leave for any length of time. Other states said freed slaves, often called freedmen, had to find employment by a certain date. Freedmen

The Freedmen's Bureau set up offices throughout the country to help newly freed slaves.

13

without proof of employment could be arrested and sent to work on a farm without pay as punishment. Some Northerners thought Southern lawmakers were using Black Codes to bring back slavery without calling it that. In 1866, Congress moved to protect the civil rights of the freedmen.

By this time, Andrew Johnson had become president following Lincoln's assassination on April 12, 1865. Johnson's home state of Tennessee had seceded, but he had remained loyal to the Union. As a former Democrat, he opposed many of the Republican Party's political goals. Johnson thought that the Southern states should be allowed back into

President Andrew Johnson

the Union as quickly as possible. In addition, he believed former leaders of the Confederacy should be allowed to serve in state governments or Congress.

Johnson clashed with Radical Republicans, a group of Republicans who wanted to deal harshly with former Confederates. The Radical Republicans were also concerned about helping the freedmen improve their conditions. Most Republicans, however, were not Radicals. They did not particularly support the rights of the freedmen. Like Johnson, they wanted to restore order and unite the country as quickly as possible. But unlike Johnson, they were not ready to give former Confederates control of the Southern states. Many of these moderate Republicans wanted to keep their party's control in Congress and state governments in the South.

Republican lawmakers believed that the national government had a duty to limit state laws that hurt blacks. In early 1866, Congress proposed the Civil Rights Act to protect the freedmen, as well as free blacks in the North.

Crowds outside the House of Representatives applaud the passage of the Civil Rights Act.

The act said all people born within the United States would be considered citizens, regardless of race. And as citizens, they had the right to make contracts and own property, among other things. The act made the Black Codes illegal, limiting the state governments' powers.

Johnson and many other Southerners opposed giving the national government more power over states. In March, Johnson vetoed the Civil Rights Act. Congress then used its constitutional power to override the veto. This meant the law went into effect without the president's approval.

16

Even though the act passed in the end, Johnson angered both Radical and moderate Republicans when he rejected the Civil Rights Act. For the next two years, the moderates worked with Radicals to shape Reconstruction to fit their plan. Johnson had few friends in Congress who would help him pursue his own goals for Reconstruction.

After the first Civil Rights Act passed in 1866, four other civil rights laws were passed in the next nine years. An illustration appeared in Harper's Weekly *after the Civil Rights Act of 1871 became a law.*

THE 14TH AMENDMENT

The Civil Rights Act offered freedmen some legal protection. But many Republicans wanted to address civil rights in a constitutional amendment. A special committee of members from both the House and Senate met to shape this amendment.

The 14th Amendment had five proposed sections. The first section said the states could not "make or enforce any law which shall abridge the privileges and immunities of citizens of the United States." All Americans had privileges, or the right to do certain things. Immunities were activities they could not be forced to do. To avoid opposition to the amendment, the lawmakers decided not to list the specific privileges and

A meeting to create the 14th Amendment

immunities that the amendment would cover. They knew Americans had many different views on laws and rights for blacks, and they wanted to win as much support as possible for the amendment. The U.S. courts would define those rights on a case-by-case basis.

Section 1 also said that no state could take away a person's "life, liberty or property without due process of the law, nor deny to any person ... equal protection of the laws." "Due process" means a government must follow its own laws when it deals with citizens. Citizens must know in advance what these laws are. "Equal protection" means the laws are applied to everyone in the same way.

Section 2 dealt with suffrage—the right to vote. At the time, most states let only white males vote. Women could not vote in any state, and only a few Northern states let blacks vote. The 14th Amendment said all males over 21, except Native Americans, had suffrage. If a state tried to keep some people from voting, it faced a penalty. The number of representatives from each state is based on

African-Americans vote in Washington, D.C., in 1867.

population. A state would lose a share of its members in the House of Representatives if it denied suffrage to blacks. So if black voters made up 10 percent of the male citizens in a state, then that state would lose 10 percent of its House members.

The amendment's third section concerned people who had supported the Confederacy during the Civil War. They would not be allowed to vote in elections for the presidency or the House of Representatives until after July 4, 1870.

Section 4 dealt with the debt of the Southern states. The Confederacy had borrowed money from Europeans and its own citizens to fight the war. The 14th Amendment said the debts would not be repaid by the United States or individual states. The creditors would be forced to take a loss on their loans. This section also said people who had owned slaves during the war could not try to seek any money to make up for the loss of their slaves.

The last section gave Congress the power to pass any laws needed to carry out the first four sections.

The special committee also proposed two related laws. One law said that once a former Confederate state ratified the amendment and changed its laws to fit its requirements, it could rejoin the Union. First, though, the 14th Amendment had to be added to the Constitution.

A second law prevented former members of the Confederate government and military from serving in the U.S. government. This also applied to former Union officials who had helped the Confederacy.

DEBATING THE AMENDMENT

In May 1866, Congress began fiercely debating the proposed 14th Amendment. Different parts of the amendment upset different people. Some lawmakers thought the first section gave the U.S. government too

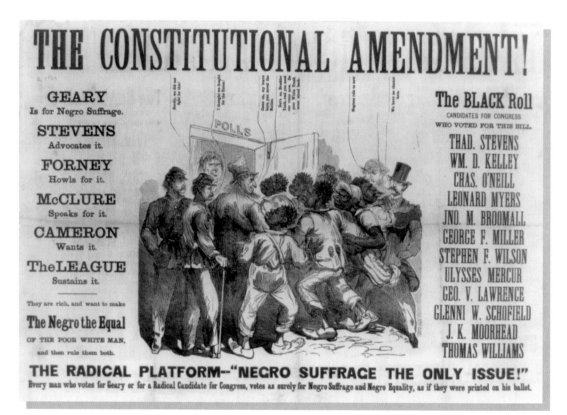

A Democratic campaign poster from 1866 delivered a racist message against suffrage for blacks.

much power over the states. But that was exactly the goal of Radical Republicans. They believed the national government should force the states to get rid of Black Codes. However, some Radicals were not happy with Section 2, which dealt with suffrage. They wanted to declare more clearly that blacks had a right to vote and not leave states any chance to deny it.

Others argued about Section 3. Some Democrats and moderate Republicans thought it was unfair to deny some Southerners the right to vote. The leading Radical Republican in the House of Representatives, Thaddeus Stevens of Pennsylvania, strongly argued for keeping the

Thaddeus Stevens

limits: "Not only to 1870, but to 18070, every rebel ... should be prevented from exercising any power in this government. That, even, would be too mild a punishment for them."

During their debates, the lawmakers made some changes to the committee's work. The first section was changed to say that everyone born in the United States or naturalized in the country was a U.S. citizen, as well as a citizen of the state where they lived. This was the first time the U.S. government had defined who was a U.S. citizen.

Congress also lifted restrictions in Section 3 and allowed all Southerners the right to vote immediately. Former Southern officials, however, faced limits. Officials who had served in the U.S. government before the Civil War and sworn to uphold the Constitution could no longer hold a national or state office if they had supported the Confederacy during the war. Congress could make exceptions in individual cases.

In June 1866, Congress voted to approve this new

version of the 14th Amendment. Congress did not pass the law, however, that required Southern states to ratify the amendment before they could re-enter the Union.

The debates continued outside of Congress. Some Radical Republicans attacked the 14th Amendment. They thought it did not punish the Southern states enough.

Wendell Phillips was the leader of the antislavery movement.

Some said it should have directly prevented Southern states from denying freedmen the right to vote. Wendell Phillips had long fought for equal rights for blacks. He called the amendment "a fatal and total surrender" to moderates and Democrats.

25

JOHNSON AND THE RADICALS

President Johnson continued to make enemies out of the Republicans. In the spring of 1866, he spoke out against the 14th Amendment. Johnson did not want to punish the former Confederate leaders by preventing them from holding political offices. Also, like some lawmakers, he thought the amendment took away the states' rights to have the kinds of laws they wanted. He did not want the national government to place new limits on the states.

In fact, Johnson did not think it was right for Congress to propose any new amendments. After all, the former Confederate states still did not have any members in the House or Senate. The president wanted Congress to let the Southern states re-enter the Union, elect representatives and senators, and then vote on new amendments.

In the fall, all the seats in the House and one-third of the Senate seats would be up for election. Johnson announced that he would not support the campaign of any

President Johnson traveled to Chicago, Illinois, and back to Washington, D.C., campaigning for candidates who opposed the 14th Amendment.

lawmakers who had voted for the 14th Amendment. Once again, Johnson angered moderate Republicans, who had supported the amendment and thought it was fair. The campaign of 1866 gave voters a chance to show what they thought about the amendment. If they opposed it, they could vote for the candidates Johnson supported. If they liked the amendment, they could reelect the members of Congress who had backed it.

In July, a violent event in New Orleans seemed to help build popular support for the 14th Amendment and the Republicans. A mob of white men, including some Democrats and former Confederate soldiers, attacked a political meeting of African-Americans and white suffrage supporters. Several dozen people were killed, most of them blacks. One man at the scene later said, "I ... saw the people on the fences with their [guns] waiting to shoot anybody

Local police did nothing to stop the fighting in the New Orleans riot.

who would show themselves, and I saw the police shoot many colored people who attempted to escape."

Many Northern voters felt that Johnson's efforts to help the former Confederate states had played a role in the killings. They thought that Southern lawmakers believed they could treat blacks unfairly and not be punished. In addition, the South did not seem to have any regrets for seceding from the Union and sparking the Civil War.

More people in the North were now willing to let Congress pursue Reconstruction as it chose. They rejected Johnson's efforts to weaken the power of the moderate and Radical Republicans. After the election of 1866, the Republicans had firm control of the Reconstruction process.

AFRICAN-AMERICAN SUFFRAGE

By the election of 1866, several states had already ratified the 14th Amendment. Southern states, however, rejected the amendment. The next year, Congress passed the Reconstruction Act. The law said that Southern states could not rejoin the Union until they ratified the 14th Amendment and changed their laws to match it.

The Reconstruction Act also divided the former Confederate states into five regions. Each one was ruled by a military governor. The military would be in control in the South until the states wrote new constitutions and Congress approved them. Only then could the states send lawmakers to Congress.

In July 1868, the 14th Amendment went into effect. By this time, lawmakers in eight former Confederate states had decided to ratify the amendment.

Meanwhile, Congress continued to battle with President Johnson. The president often vetoed

The Reconstruction Act divided the former Confederacy into five military districts.

Reconstruction laws that he thought were unconstitutional.

Congress then voted to override his vetoes. The conflict

led Congress to do something it had never done before—

impeach a president. In the impeachment process, the

House of Representatives accuses a government official of

31

crimes. The Senate then decides whether or not the person is guilty and should be removed from office.

The Radical Republicans had designed a law to set up President Johnson for impeachment. The law limited his power to fire members of his Cabinet. As expected, Johnson broke the law. Early in 1868, Johnson dismissed his secretary of war, Edwin M. Stanton, who had ceased to support the president. The House responded with impeachment proceedings.

Johnson argued that the law, called the Tenure of

The 1868 impeachment trial of Andrew Johnson in the U.S. Senate

Office Act, was unconstitutional, so he did not have to follow it. By just one vote, the Senate decided that Johnson could remain president. By this time, however, Johnson had lost any influence he once had. Neither party wanted him to run for president in the upcoming election. In 1868, the Republicans backed Ulysses S. Grant, and he easily won.

But voting numbers in the 1868 election worried some Republican lawmakers. In the North, their party did not do as well as it had in the past. In the South, the support of black voters had helped Grant win. But despite being penalized by losing representatives, some Southern states still had not given blacks the right to vote. Republicans feared that Southern state governments would continue to deny blacks their suffrage. Many thought the national government needed to guarantee blacks the right to vote across the country with a new constitutional amendment.

For some Republicans, granting suffrage was a political issue. The lawmakers assumed that blacks with the newly won right to vote would support the party that had helped them—the Republicans. That same support might help the Republicans defeat the Democrats in upcoming elections.

The 15th Amendment grew out of these concerns. The amendment said the U.S. government and the states could not deny someone the right to vote because of their race or color, or because they had once been a slave.

Some Northern lawmakers, however, opposed this amendment. Many Northern states did not let their black citizens vote. Lawmakers feared they would lose the support of white racist voters in the North if they called for African-American suffrage. Other members of Congress again talked about states' rights. They did not think the national government should tell the states who could vote in state elections. And lawmakers from Western states with large Asian populations, such as California, opposed the amendment because it gave members of any race the right to vote. These lawmakers did not want Asians to vote.

The original 15th Amendment proposal

Despite these arguments, Congress passed the 15th Amendment on February 26, 1869. The next year, the amendment became part of the Constitution.

AFTER RECONSTRUCTION

Reconstruction ended in 1877. The U.S. military pulled out of the South, and Democrats took back control of the government in many Southern states. By this time, the 13th Amendment had little effect in the day-to-day lives of Americans. Slavery was clearly over and would never return. But the other two amendments continued to play a part in U.S. politics and society.

States kept trying to pass laws that limited the rights of blacks. In 1873, part of the 14th Amendment was examined by the U.S. Supreme Court, the most powerful in the United States. The court helps define what the Constitution and its amendments mean.

The Supreme Court said the "privileges and immunities" mentioned in the 14th Amendment did not prevent states from controlling most civil rights. Later, the court said private groups could also deny a person's rights, since they were not connected to the states.

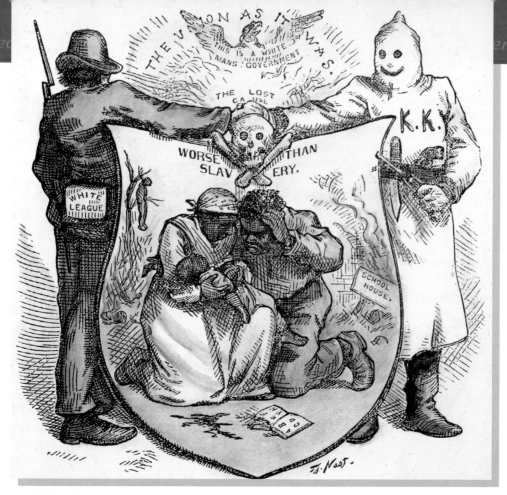

An 1874 political cartoon by Thomas Nast implies that the racial abuse that African-Americans suffered after the Civil War was worse than slavery.

In 1896, the Supreme Court heard a legal case called Plessy v. Ferguson. This case dealt with segregation between whites and blacks in public places. In their ruling, the court said the "equal protection" part of the 14th Amendment also had limits. This ruling was called the "separate but equal doctrine." It said states could legally

37

segregate blacks and whites in public places. For example, a state could set up one school system for black children and another for whites, as long they offered equal education. In practice, however, segregated schools and other services were rarely equal. Blacks received much worse treatment than whites.

Southern states also found ways to avoid the 15th Amendment. Some states began to require that voters pay a tax before they could vote. Other states required voters to

Classrooms in schools for black children were often overcrowded.

An 1874 political cartoon shows a white racist trying to keep a black man from voting with the threat of his gun.

take literacy tests to prove they could read and write. These laws applied to all voters, but they affected many more blacks than whites. Recently freed slaves and their children were often poor and uneducated. In addition, the literacy tests were unfair. Black voters would be given a much more difficult passage to read than white voters.

Blacks lacked the money to challenge these voter laws in court. Even if they did, the legal system was not color blind. Writing about the 14th and 15th Amendments, one Southern newspaper said they "may stand forever; but we intend ... to make them dead letters on the [law] books."

Segregated public services remained legal in the United States until the 1950s. The Supreme Court changed its views on equal protection and said "separate but equal" was not constitutional. It took several more years, however, for all Southern states to end segregation. In 1965, Congress acted to address limits on suffrage. The Voting Rights Act ended poll taxes and literacy tests. It was the first major law that the Supreme Court supported to protect the rights that blacks had earned almost 100 years before.

Today, the 14th Amendment is one of the most important parts of the Constitution. The issues of equal

Peaceful protests in the early 1960s helped bring about improved civil rights for blacks.

protection and due process are often debated in courts. Some Americans still think the amendment unfairly gives the national government too much power over the states. Yet the amendment has also helped many people of all races receive equal treatment, just as Congress had intended.

GLOSSARY

abolition—the immediate end of something, such as slavery

amendment—a formal change made to a law or legal document, such as a constitution

Cabinet—a president's group of advisers who are the heads of government departments

civil rights—legal rights guaranteed to every citizen of a country relating to such things as voting and receiving equal treatment

Congress—the branch of the U.S. government that makes laws, consisting of the House of Representatives and the Senate

constitutional—allowed under a government's constitution

naturalized—made a citizen of a country or state although born in a different country

racist—a person who judges people based on their race and thinks his or her own race is better than all others

segregate—to separate groups of people based on their race

vetoed—rejected a proposed law

DID YOU KNOW?

- The Civil Rights Bill of 1866 was the first U.S. law ever to take effect after Congress overrode a president's veto.

- Andrew Johnson was the first U.S. president to face an impeachment trial. After he left office, the U.S. Supreme Court agreed with him that the law he supposedly broke was unconstitutional.

- Since Reconstruction, the Democratic and Republican parties have changed some of their basic beliefs. The Republicans today are less willing to use the power of the national government to limit the rights of state governments. Democrats now believe the national government should play a larger role in shaping the economy and protecting equal rights.

- Since 1789, members of Congress have proposed more than 10,000 amendments to the Constitution. Only 27 of them have been approved by Congress and ratified by the states. The last amendment was added in 1992. It prevents current members of Congress from giving themselves pay raises.

IMPORTANT DATES

Timeline

1865	In January, Congress votes for the 13th Amendment; in April, the Civil War ends, President Lincoln is shot, and Andrew Johnson takes his place; in December, the 13th Amendment is added to the Constitution.
1866	Congress votes for the 14th Amendment and passes the Reconstruction Act.
1868	In the spring, Congress tries to impeach President Johnson; in July, the 14th Amendment becomes part of the Constitution; in November, Ulysses S. Grant is elected president.
1869	Congress approves the 15th Amendment.
1870	The 15th Amendment becomes part of the Constitution.
1877	Reconstruction ends.

IMPORTANT PEOPLE

ABRAHAM LINCOLN (1809–1865)
U.S. president who fought the Civil War to keep the Union whole and later freed many slaves

ANDREW JOHNSON (1808–1875)
U.S. president during the first part of Reconstruction who opposed the 14th Amendment

ROBERT E. LEE (1807–1870)
Confederate general who surrendered in 1865, ending the Civil War

THADDEUS STEVENS (1792–1868)
Member of the House of Representatives from Pennsylvania and a leader of the Radical Republicans in Congress

ULYSSES S. GRANT (1822–1885)
Union general elected U.S. president in 1868

WENDELL PHILLIPS (1811–1884)
A leader of the effort to abolish slavery and strong supporter of civil rights for freedmen

WANT TO KNOW MORE?

At the Library

Anderson, Dale. *The Aftermath of the Civil War.* Milwaukee: World
Almanac Library, 2004.

Greene, Meg. *Into the Land of Freedom: African Americans in Reconstruction.*
Minneapolis: Lerner Publications, 2004.

Hudson, David, Jr. *The Fourteenth Amendment: Equal Protection Under the
Law.* Berkeley Heights, N.J.: Enslow Publishers, 2002.

Sobel, Syl. *The U.S. Constitution and You.* Hauppauge, N.Y.: Barron's
Educational Series, Inc., 2001.

On the Web

For more information on *The Reconstruction Amendments,* use FactHound
to track down Web sites related to this book.

1. Go to *www.facthound.com*

2. Type in a search word related to this book
or this book ID: 0756516366

3. Click on the *Fetch It* button.

Your trusty FactHound will fetch the best Web sites for you!

On the Road

Andrew Johnson National Historic Site
121 Monument Ave.
Greeneville, TN 37743-5552
423/638-3551
The Tennessee home of the 17th president

U.S. Supreme Court
One First Street, N.E.
Washington, DC 20543
202/479-3211
The highest court in the United States

Look for more We the People books about this era:

The Assassination of Abraham Lincoln
ISBN 0-7565-0678-6

The Battle of Gettysburg
ISBN 0-7565-0098-2

Battle of the Ironclads
ISBN 0-7565-1628-5

The Carpetbaggers
ISBN 0-7565-0834-7

The Emancipation Proclamation
ISBN 0-7565-0209-8

Fort Sumter
ISBN 0-7565-1629-3

The Gettysburg Address
ISBN 0-7565-1271-9

Great Women of the Civil War
ISBN 0-7565-0839-8

The Lincoln–Douglas Debates
ISBN 0-7565-1632-3

The Missouri Compromise
ISBN 0-7565-1634-X

Surrender at Appomattox
ISBN 0-7565-1626-9

The Underground Railroad
ISBN 0-7565-0102-4

A complete list of We the People titles is available on our Web site:
www.compasspointbooks.com

INDEX

About the Author

Michael Burgan is a freelance writer of books for children and adults. A history graduate of the University of Connecticut, he has written more than 90 fiction and nonfiction children's books. For adult audiences, he has written news articles, essays, and plays. Michael Burgan is a recipient of an Educational Press Association of America award.